WHO SAID HANDWRITING HAD TO BE BORING?

Designed for kids who are tired of boring ABC practice pages.

Authored by April Geer

LET'S DO SOME QUICK WARM-UP DRILLS

But do take your time on these first couple pages.
A good warm-up helps to set you up for success.

Let's just make sure you're forming the letters correctly. Trace the uppercase letters, making sure to follow the numbers and arrows.

A B C D E
F G H I J
K L M N
O P Q R S
T U V W
X Y Z

Let's just make sure you're forming the letters correctly. Trace the lowercase letters, making sure to follow the numbers and arrows.

a b c d e
f g h i j
k l m n
o p q r s
t u v w
x y z

Now trace the alphabet - making sure to form each letter correctly.

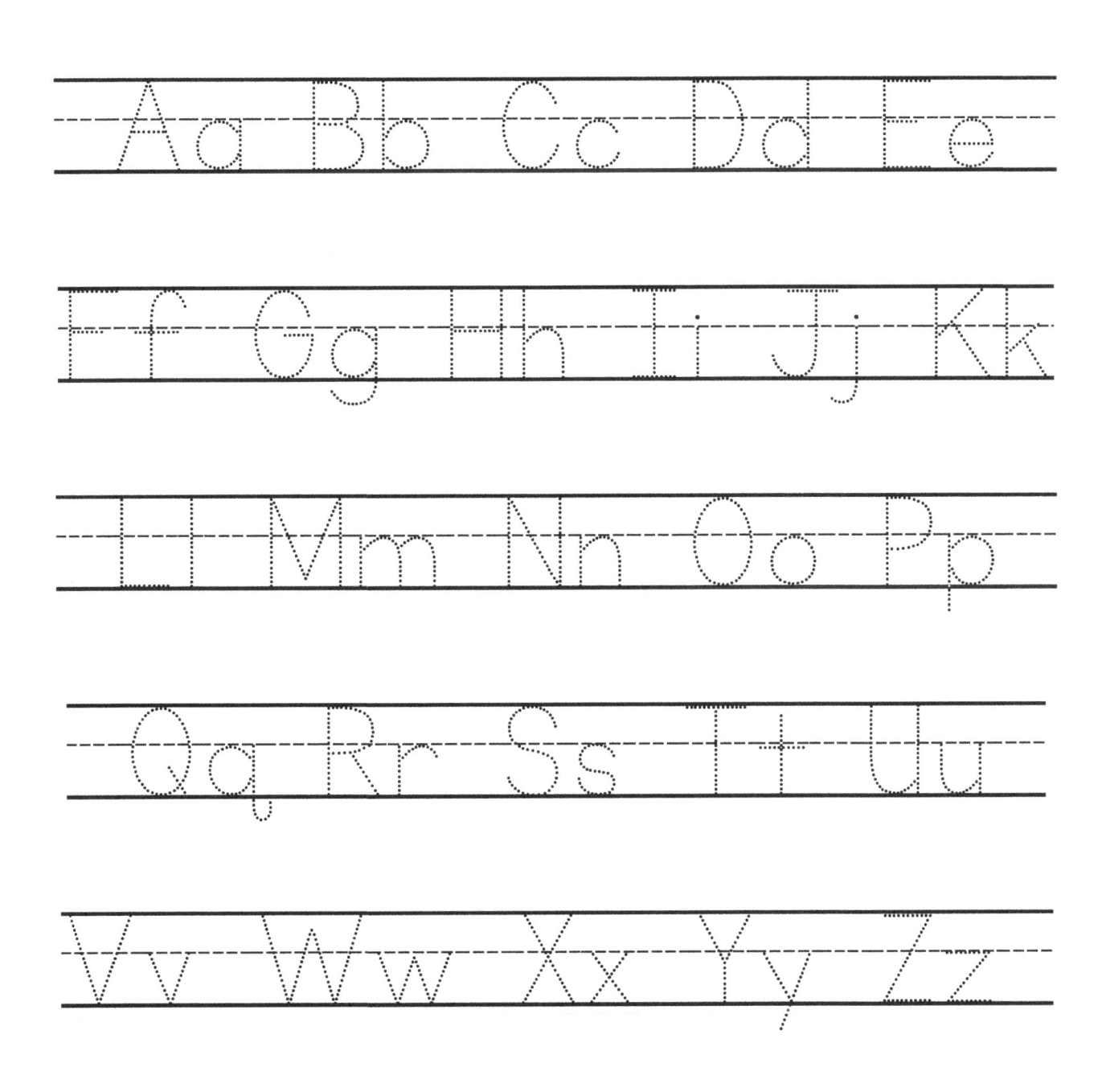

Aa Bb Cc Dd Ee

Ff Gg Hh Ii Jj Kk

Ll Mm Nn Oo Pp

Qq Rr Ss Tt Uu

Vv Ww Xx Yy Zz

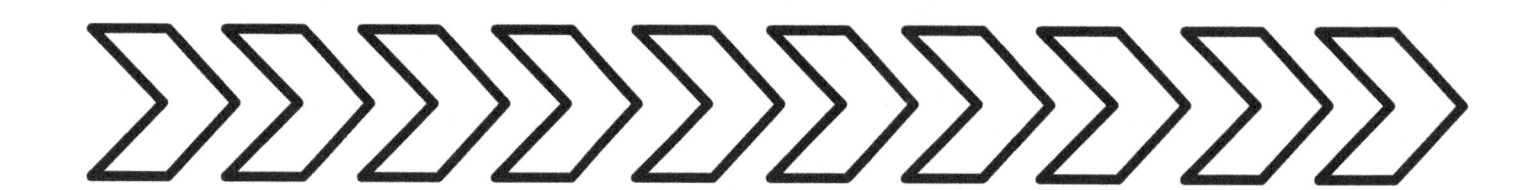

WARM-UP COMPLETE

Now you're ready for the good stuff!

Take your time and let the pencil flow smoothly across each page. Take a nice deep break after each page and observe your progress.

"It's hard to beat a person who never gives up." —Babe Ruth

Trace the quote:

"It's hard to beat a person who never gives up." - Babe Ruth.

Now it's your turn:

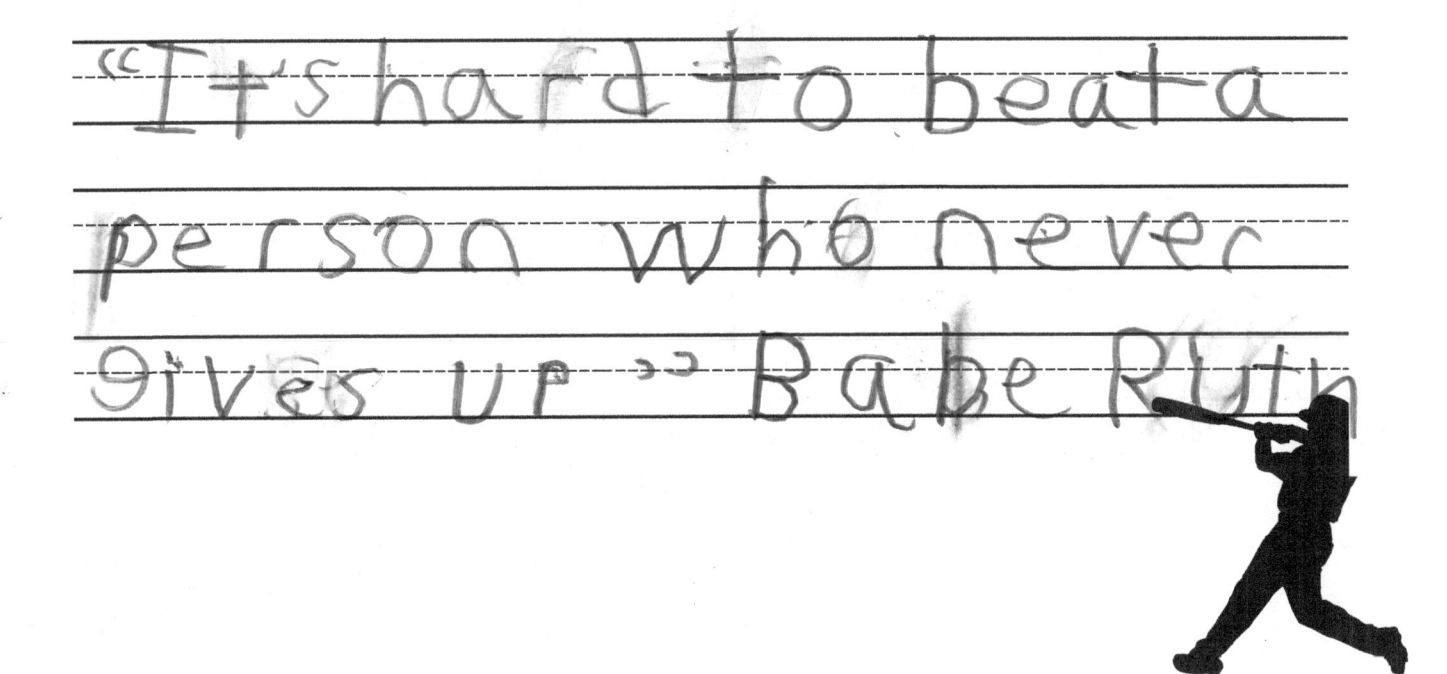

"It's hard to beat a person who never gives up." Babe Ruth

DID YOU KNOW?

Tomatoes and avocados are actually fruits, not vegetables.

Trace the fact:

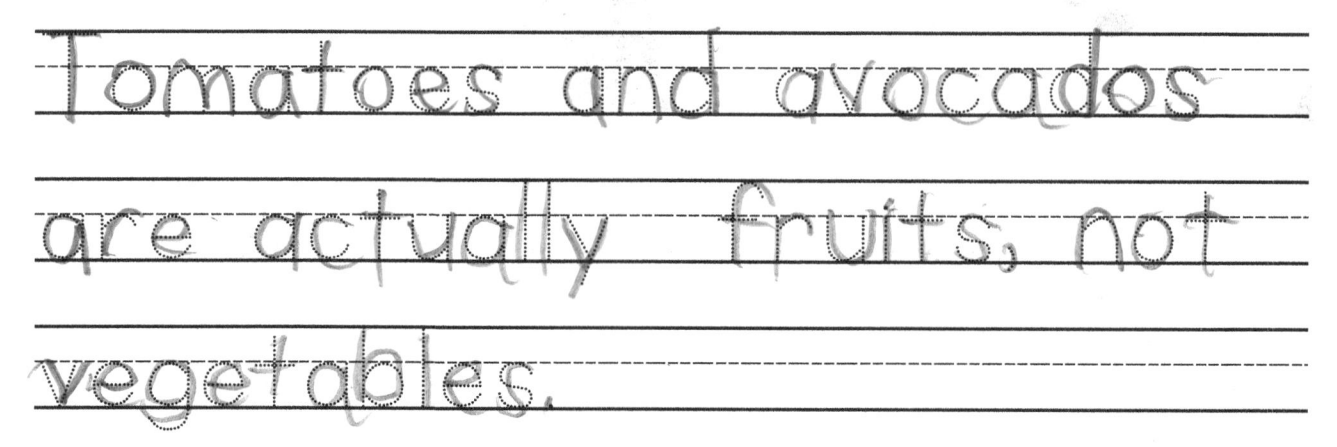

Tomatoes and avocados
are actually fruits, not
vegetables.

Now it's your turn:

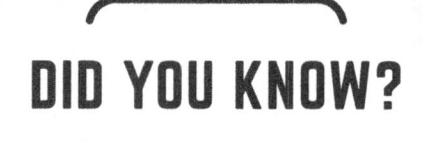

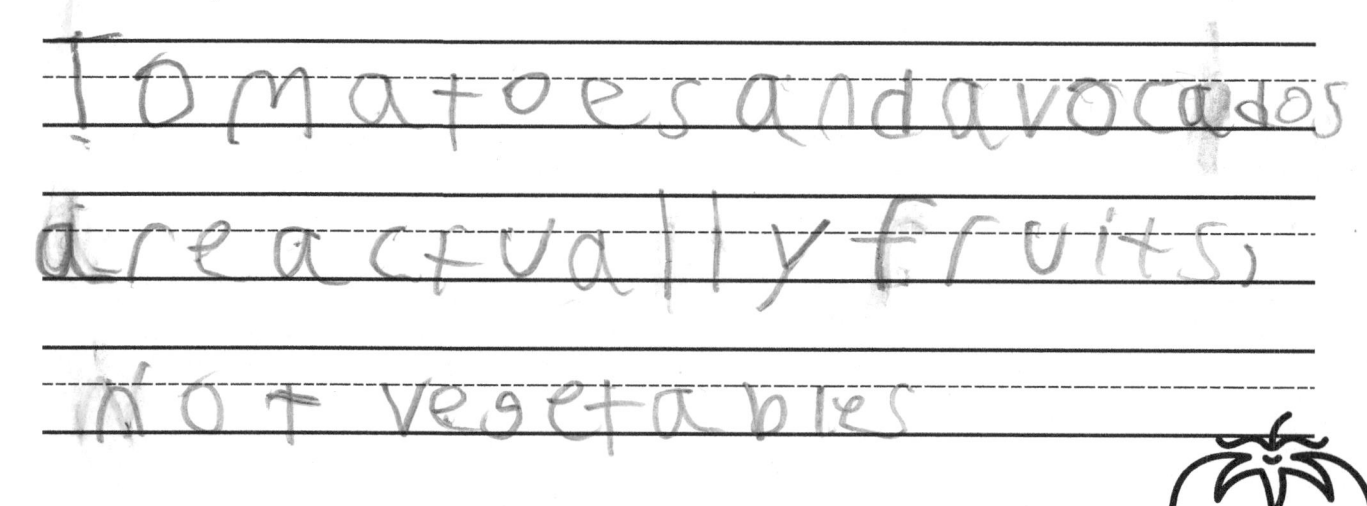

Tomatoesandavocados
areactuallyfruits,
not vegetables

What do you call a pig that knows karate?
A pork chop!

Trace the joke:

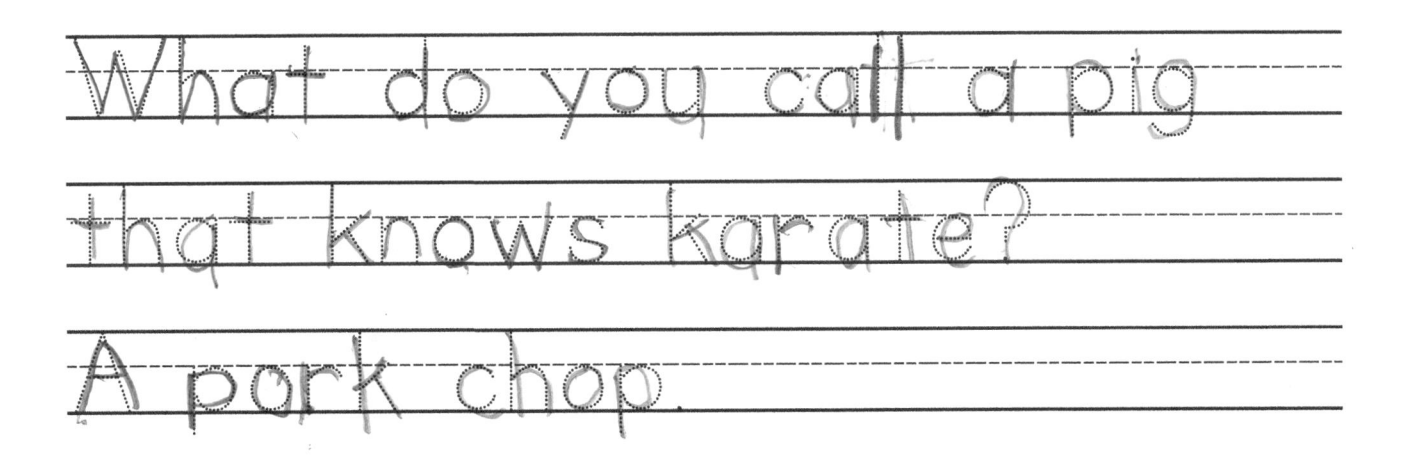

What do you call a pig
that knows karate?
A pork chop.

Now it's your turn:

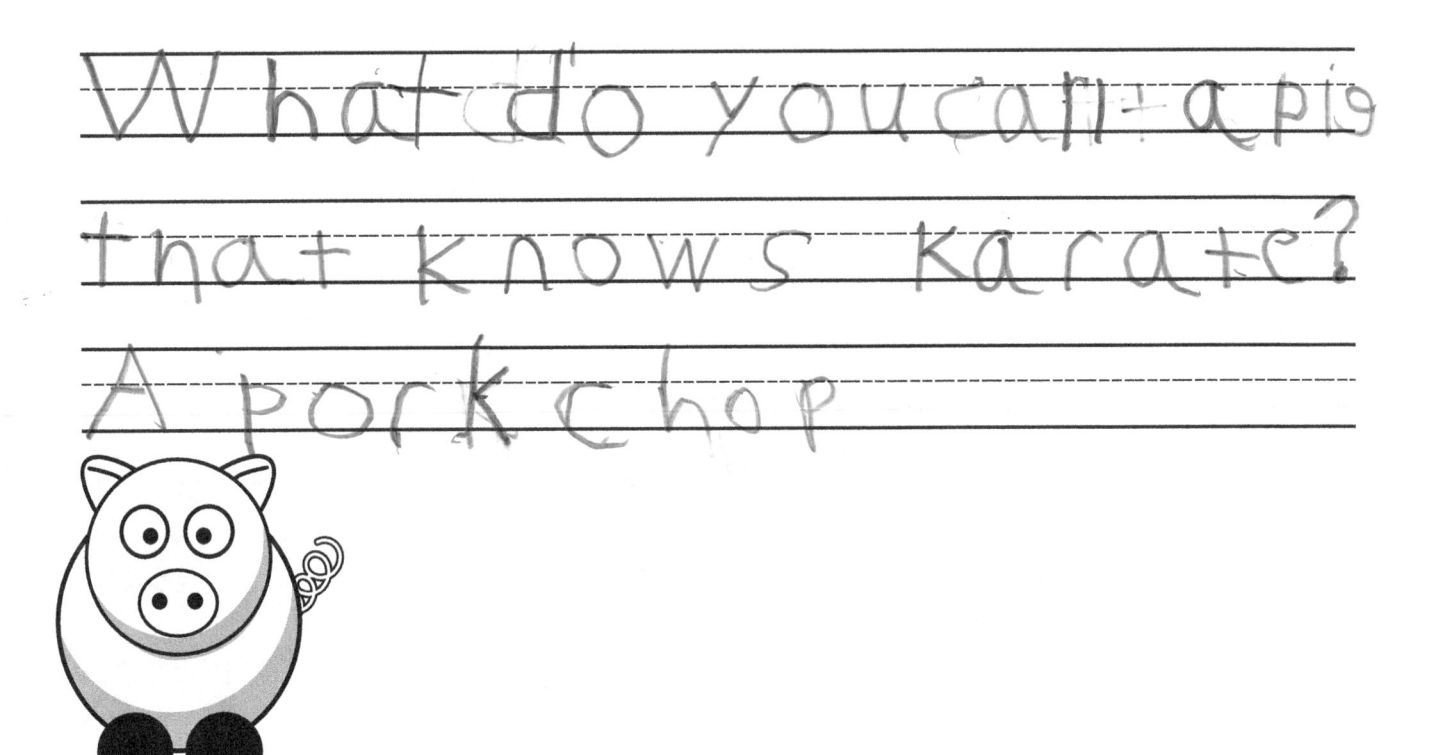

What do you call a pig
that knows karate?
A pork chop

"Never say never because limits, like fears, are often just an illusion."
—Michael Jordan

Trace the quote:

"Never say never because limits, like fears, are often just an illusion."
—Michael Jordan

Now it's your turn:

DID YOU KNOW?

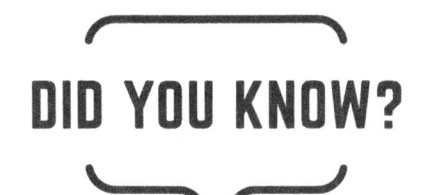

Because bananas contain potassium, they are radioactive.

Trace the fact:

Because bananas contain potassium, they are radioactive.

Now it's your turn:

Where do cows go on Friday nights?
They go to the moo-vies!

Trace the joke:

Where do cows go on
Friday nights?
They go to the moo-vies!

Now it's your turn:

"Talent without working hard is nothing."
—Cristiano Ronaldo

Trace the quote:

"Talent without working hard is nothing."
Christian Ronaldo

Now it's your turn:

DID YOU KNOW?

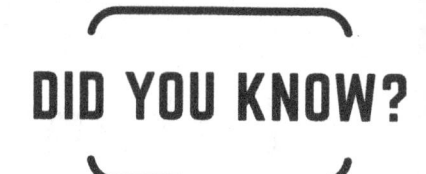

Strawberries are the only fruits with their seeds on the outside.

Trace the fact:

Strawberries are the only fruits with their seeds on the outside.

Now it's your turn:

What time is it when the clock strikes 13?
Time to get a new clock.

Trace the joke:

What time is it when the
clock strikes 13?
Time to get a new clock.

Now it's your turn:

"Courage doesn't mean you don't get afraid. Courage means you don't let fear stop you." —Bethany Hamilton

Trace the quote:

"Courage doesn't mean you don't get afraid. Courage means you don't let fear stop you." —Bethany Hamilton

Now it's your turn:

> **DID YOU KNOW?**

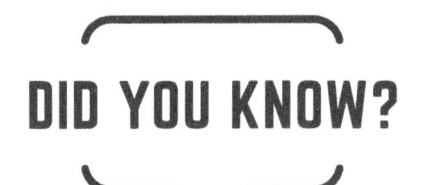

Because of gravity, you would weigh less on the moon than on Earth.

Trace the fact:

Because of gravity, you would weigh less on the moon than on Earth.

Now it's your turn:

How does a cucumber become a pickle?
It goes through a jarring experience.

Trace the joke:

How does a cucumber
become a pickle?
It goes through a jarring
experience.

Now it's your turn:

"It's not whether you get knocked down; it's whether you get up."
—Vince Lombardi

Trace the quote:

It's not whether you get knocked down; It's whether you get up."
—Vince Lombardi

Now it's your turn:

DID YOU KNOW?

White is not actually a color, but the absence of all colors.

Trace the fact:

White is not actually a color, but the absence of all colors.

Now it's your turn:

Why did the dinosaur cross the road?
Because the chicken wasn't born yet.

Trace the joke:

Why did the dinosaur cross
te road?
Because the chicken wasn't
born yet.

Now it's your turn:

"The only way to prove that you're a good sport is to lose." —Ernie Banks

Trace the quote:

"The only way to prove that you're a good sport is to lose." —Ernie Banks

Now it's your turn:

DID YOU KNOW?

If you folded a piece of paper 42 times, it would be thick enough to reach the moon.

Trace the fact:

If you folded a piece of
paper 42 times, it would be
thick enough to reach the
moon.

Now it's your turn:

How does a scientist freshen her breath?
With experi-mints.

Trace the joke:

How does a scientist
freshen her breath?
With experi-mints.

Now it's your turn:

"Make sure your worst enemy doesn't live between your own two ears." —Laird Hamilton

Trace the quote:

"Make sure your worst
enemy doesn't live
between your own two
ears." —Laird Hamilton

Now it's your turn:

DID YOU KNOW?

The average cloud weighs an estimated 1.1 million pounds.

Trace the fact:

The average cloud weighs an estimated 1.1 million pounds.

Now it's your turn:

What falls in the winter but never gets hurt?
Snow.

Trace the joke:

What falls in the winter
but never gets hurt?
Snow.

Now it's your turn:

"If something stands between you and your success, move it. Never be denied."
—Dwayne "The Rock" Johnson

Trace the quote:

"If something stands between you and your success, move it. Never be denied."
—Dwayne "The Rock" Johnson

Now it's your turn:

DID YOU KNOW?

A million seconds is about 12 days while a billion seconds is about 32 years.

Trace the fact:

A million seconds is about 12 days, while a billion seconds is about 32 years.

Now it's your turn:

What did the left eye say to the right eye?
Between us, something smells.

Trace the joke:

What did the left eye say to
the right eye?
Between us, something smells.

Now it's your turn:

"If you can't outplay them, outwork them."
—Ben Hogan

Trace the quote:

"If you can't outplay
them, outwork them."
—Ben Hogan

Now it's your turn:

DID YOU KNOW?

Scientists believe that there are more than 10 million different kinds of life forms on earth.

Trace the fact:

Scientists believe that there are more than 10 million different kinds of life forms on earth.

Now it's your turn:

What do snowmen eat for breakfast?
Frosted Flakes.

Trace the joke:

What do snowmen eat
for breakfast?
Frosted Flakes.

Now it's your turn:

"If you fail to prepare, you're prepared to fail."
—Mark Spitz

Trace the quote:

"If you fail to prepare,
you're prepared to fail."
—Mark Spitz

Now it's your turn:

DID YOU KNOW?

Herring fish communicate with each other through farts.

Trace the fact:

Herring Fish communicate with each other through farts.

Now it's your turn:

Why did the robber jump in the shower?
He wanted to make a clean getaway.

Trace the joke:

Why did the robber jump in
the shower?
He wanted to make a clean
getaway.

Now it's your turn:

"You can't put a limit on anything. The more you dream, the farther you get." —Michael Phelps

Trace the quote:

"You can't put a limit on anything. The more you dream, the farther you get." —Michael Phelps

Now it's your turn:

DID YOU KNOW?

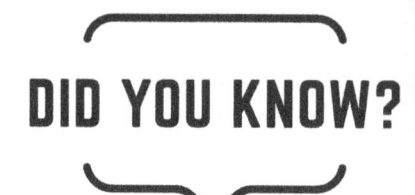

Kangaroos can not walk backwards.

Trace the fact:

Kangaroos can not
walk backwards.

Now it's your turn:

Why are peppers the best at archery?
Because they habanero!

Trace the joke:

Why are peppers the

best at archery?

Because they habanero!

Now it's your turn:

"It is not the size of a man but the size of his heart that matters."
—Evander Holyfield

Trace the quote:

"It is not the size of a
man but the size of his
heart that matters."
—Evander Holyfield

Now it's your turn:

DID YOU KNOW?

It takes about 50 licks to finish just one scoop of ice cream.

Trace the fact:

It takes about 50 licks to finish just one scoop of ice cream.

Now it's your turn:

Why can't you tell a joke to an egg?
It might crack up!

Trace the joke:

Why can't you tell a

joke to an egg?

It might crack up!

Now it's your turn:

"Always make a total effort, even when the odds are against you."
—Arnold Palmer

Trace the quote:

"Always make a total effort, even when the odds are against you."
—Arnold Palmer

Now it's your turn:

DID YOU KNOW?

North Korea and Cuba are the only places in the world you can't buy Coca Cola.

Trace the fact:

North Korea and Cuba are
the only places in the world
you can't buy Coca Cola.

Now it's your turn:

Where do elephants pack their clothes?
In their trunks!

HA HA

Trace the joke:

Where do elephants pack
their clothes?
In their trunks!

Now it's your turn:

"The only way to prove that you're a good sport is to lose."
—Ernie Banks

Trace the quote:

"The only way to prove that you're a good sport is to lose."
—Ernie Banks

Now it's your turn:

DID YOU KNOW?

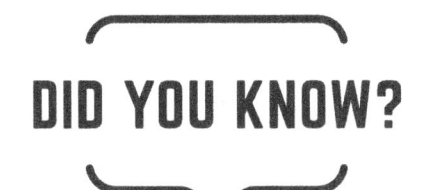

Your nose gets warmer when you lie.

Trace the fact:

Your nose gets warmer
when you lie.

Now it's your turn:

Which bird is always out of breath?
A puffin!

Trace the joke:

Which bird is always out
of breath?
A puffin!

Now it's your turn:

"A champion is afraid of losing. Everyone else is afraid of winning."
—Billie Jean King

Trace the quote:

"A champion is afraid of
losing. Everyone else is
afraid of winning."
—Billie Jean King

Now it's your turn:

DID YOU KNOW?

Insects have been around for about 350 million years.

Trace the quote:

Insects have been
around for about 350
million years.

Now it's your turn:

What did the duck say after she bought chapstick?
Put it on my bill!

Trace the joke:

What did the duck say
after she bought
chapstick?
Put it on my bill!

Now it's your turn:

"Winning isn't everything, but wanting to win is."
—Vince Lombardi

Trace the quote:

"Winning isn't everything,

but wanting to win is."

—Vince Lombardi

Now it's your turn:

DID YOU KNOW?

Scotland has more than 400 words for "snow".

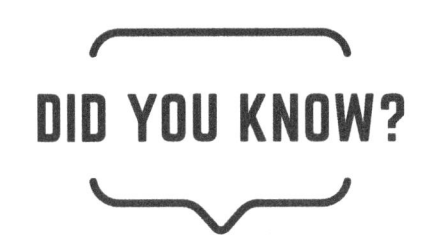

Trace the fact:

Scotland has more than
400 words for "snow".

Now it's your turn:

What did the cat say when it fell down the stairs?
Me-ow!

Trace the joke:

What did the cat say
when it fell down the
stairs?
Me-ow!

Now it's your turn:

"You can't win unless you learn how to lose." 99
—Kareem Abdul-Jabbar

Trace the quote:

"You can't win unless
you learn how to lose."
—Kareem Abdul-Jabbar

Now it's your turn:

> DID YOU KNOW?

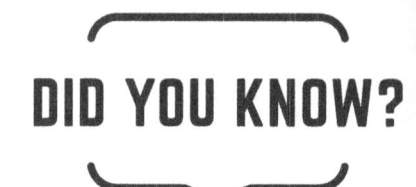

Your heart beats about 115,000 every day.

Trace the fact:

Your heart beats about
115,000 every day.

Now it's your turn:

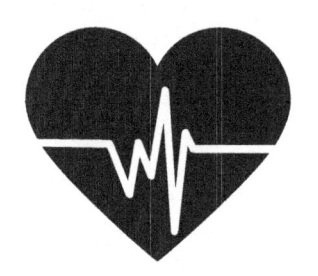

Why did the student eat his homework?
Because the teacher told him it was a piece of cake!

Trace the joke:

Why did the student eat
his homework?
Because the teacher told
him it was a piece of cake!

Now it's your turn:

"If you don't have confidence, you'll always find a way not to win."
—Carl Lewis

Trace the quote:

"If you don't have confidence, you'll always find a way not to win."
—Carl Lewis

Now it's your turn:

DID YOU KNOW?

A crab's taste buds are on their feet.

Trace the fact:

A crab's taste buds are
on their feet.

Now it's your turn:

Why did the kid cross the playground?
To get to the other slide.

Trace the joke:

Why did the kid cross
the playground?
To get to the other slide.

Now it's your turn:

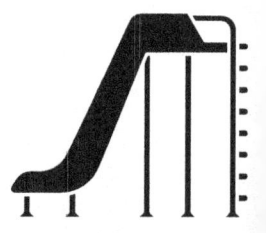

"Passion first and everything will fall into place." —Holly Holm

Trace the quote:

"Passion first and
everything will fall into
place." — Holly Holm

Now it's your turn:

DID YOU KNOW?

The human eye is comprised of about 2 million working parts.

Trace the fact:

The human eye is comprised of about 2 million working parts.

Now it's your turn:

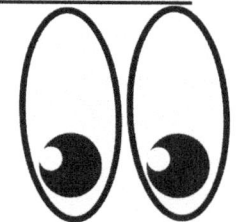

Why can't you trust an atom?
They make up everything.

Trace the joke:

Why can't you trust an

atom?

They make up everything.

Now it's your turn:

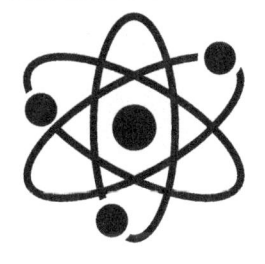

"Do not let what you can not do interfere with what you can do."
—John Wooden

Trace the quote:

"Do not let what you can not do interfere with what you can do."
—John Wooden

Now it's your turn:

DID YOU KNOW?

Dinosaur fossils have been found on all seven continents.

Trace the fact:

Dinosaur fossils have

been found on all seven

continents.

Now it's your turn:

How do you talk to a giant?
Use big words!

Trace the joke:

How do you talk to a
giant?
Use big words!

Now it's your turn:

"Set your goals high, and don't stop till you get there."
—Bo Jackson

Trace the quote:

"Set your goals high, and don't stop till you get there."
—Bo Jackson

Now it's your turn:

DID YOU KNOW?

The Empire State Building gets struck by lightning an average of 25 times a year.

Trace the fact:

The Empire State Building gets struck by lightning an average of 25 times a year.

Now it's your turn:

How can you tell a vampire has a cold?
She starts coffin.

HA HA

Trace the joke:

How can you tell a
vampire has a cold?
She starts coffin.

Now it's your turn:

"You miss 100 percent of the shots you don't take." —Wayne Gretzky

Trace the quote:

"You miss 100 percent of
the shots you don't take."
—Wayne Gretzky

Now it's your turn:

DID YOU KNOW?

Hurricanes north of the Earth's equator spin counterclockwise.

Trace the fact:

Hurricanes north of the Earth's equator spin counterclockwise.

Now it's your turn:

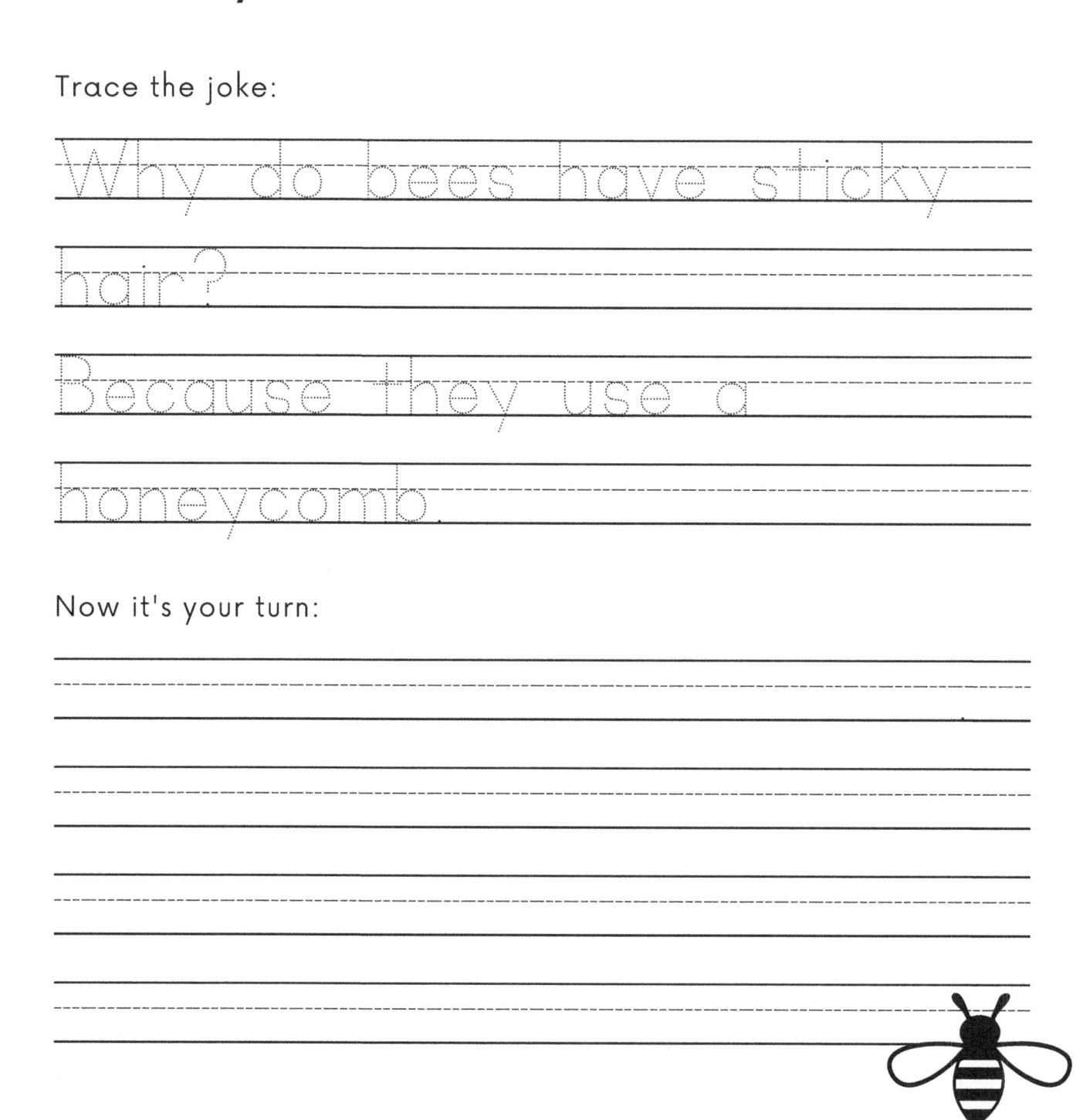

Why do bees have sticky hair?
Because they use a honeycomb.

Trace the joke:

Why do bees have sticky
hair?
Because they use a
honeycomb.

Now it's your turn:

"Champions keep playing 99 until they get it right."
—Billie Jean King

Trace the quote:

"Champions keep playing
until they get it right."
—Billie Jean King

Now it's your turn:

DID YOU KNOW?

Hurricanes south of the Earth's equator spin clockwise.

Trace the fact:

Hurricanes south of the
Earth's equator spin
clockwise.

Now it's your turn:

What did the big flower say to the little flower?
Hi, bud!

HA HA

Trace the joke:

What did the big flower
say to the little flower?
Hi, bud!

Now it's your turn:

"Push yourself again and again. Don't give an inch until the final buzzer sounds." —Larry Bird

Trace the quote:

"Push yourself again and again. Don't give an inch until the final buzzer sounds." —Larry Bird

Now it's your turn:

DID YOU KNOW?

Applesauce was the first food eaten in space.

Trace the fact:

Applesauce was the first food eaten in space.

Now it's your turn:

Why didn't the orange win the race?
It ran out of juice.

Trace the joke:

Why didn't the orange
win the race?
It ran out of juice.

Now it's your turn:

"Be humble. Be hungry. And always be the hardest worker in the room."
—Dwayne 'The Rock' Johnson

Trace the quote:

"Be humble. Be hungry. And always be the hardest worker in the room."
—Dwayne 'The Rock' Johnson

Now it's your turn:

DID YOU KNOW?

The Earth's core is as hot as the surface of the sun.

Trace the fact:

The Earth's core is as
hot as the surface of
the sun.

Now it's your turn:

What dinosaur had the best vocabulary?
The thesaurus.

Trace the joke:

What dinosaur had the
best vocabulary?
The thesaurus.

Now it's your turn:

"Start where you are. Use what you have. Do what you can." —Arthur Ashe

Trace the quote:

"Start where you are. Use what you have. Do what you can."
—Arthur Ashe

Now it's your turn:

DID YOU KNOW?

There are more stars in the universe than grains of sand on Earth.

Trace the fact:

There are more stars in
the universe than grains
of sand on Earth.

Now it's your turn:

What did the banana say to the dog?
Nothing. Bananas can't talk.

Trace the joke:

What did the banana say
to the dog?
Nothing. Bananas can't
talk.

Now it's your turn:

"No matter how good you get, you can always get better and that's the exciting part." —Tiger Woods

Trace the quote:

"No matter how good you get, you can always get better and that's the exciting part." —Tiger Woods

Now it's your turn:

The colors of a rainbow always appear in the same order.

DID YOU KNOW?

Trace the fact:

The colors of a rainbow
always appear in the
same order.

Now it's your turn:

What do you call an old snowman?
Water.

Trace the joke:

What do you call an

old snowman?

Water.

Now it's your turn:

"Knowing is not enough, we must apply. Willing is not enough, we must do."
—Bruce Lee

Trace the quote:

"Knowing is not enough, we must apply. Willing is not enough, we must do."
—Bruce Lee

Now it's your turn:

Apples float because they are one-quarter air!

DID YOU KNOW?

Trace the fact:

Apples float because
they are one-quarter air!

Now it's your turn:

How do you throw a party in space?
You planet.

Trace the joke:

How do you throw a
party in space?
You planet.

Now it's your turn:

"Nobody who gave his best ever regretted it."
—George Halas

Trace the quote:

"Nobody who gave his best ever regretted it."
—George Halas

Now it's your turn:

DID YOU KNOW?

A bolt of lightning is five times hotter than the sun.

Trace the fact:

A bolt of lightning is five times hotter than the sun.

Now it's your turn:

Why was 6 afraid of 7?
Because 7 8 9.

Trace the joke:

Why was 6 afraid of 7?

Because 7 8 9.

Now it's your turn:

"It's not wanting to win that makes you a winner; it's refusing to fail."
—Peyton Manning

Trace the quote:

"It's not wanting to win
that makes you a winner;
it's refusing to fail."
—Peyton Manning

Now it's your turn:

DID YOU KNOW?

An ostrich's eye is bigger than its brain.

Trace the fact:

An ostrich's eye is bigger than its brain.

Now it's your turn:

What time do ducks wake up?
At the quack of dawn.

HA HA

Trace the joke:

What time do ducks
wake up?
At the quack of dawn.

Now it's your turn:

"I mean, it's not important what kind of pants you were; it's how you wear them." —Ronnie Lott

Trace the quote:

"I mean, it's not important
what kind of pants you
were; it's how you wear
them." — Ronnie Lott

Now it's your turn:

Sloths are strong swimmers, especially good at the backstroke.

DID YOU KNOW?

Trace the fact:

Sloths are strong
swimmers, especially
good at the backstroke.

Now it's your turn:

Why did Superman flush the toilet?
Because it was his doody.

Trace the joke:

Why did Superman flush
the toilet?
Because it was his doody.

Now it's your turn:

"The best motivation always comes from within."
—Michael Johnson

Trace the quote:

"The best motivation
always comes from within."
—Michael Johnson

Now it's your turn:

DID YOU KNOW?

You can't breathe and swallow at the same time.

Trace the fact:

You can't breathe and
swallow at the same
time.

Now it's your turn:

Why did the giraffe get bad grades?
She had her head in the clouds.

Trace the joke:

Why did the giraffe get
bad grades?
She had her head in the
clouds.

Now it's your turn:

"I don't count my situps." I only start counting once it starts hurting."
—Muhammad Ali

Trace the quote:

"I don't count my situps.
I only start counting
once it starts hurting."
—Muhammad Ali

Now it's your turn:

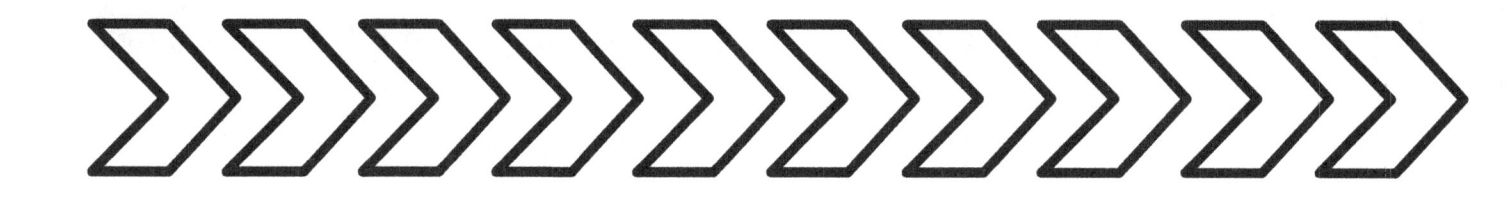

YOU DID IT!

Wow, way to put the hard work in! Congratulations for completing this work - your handwriting surely thanks you for how much more polished it has become after all that practice.

Made in the USA
Monee, IL
29 June 2023